Welcome to St Martin-in-the-Fields, an architectural jewel sitting at the corner of one of the world's most famous city squares. St Martin's is a place of encounter: in its worship, between God and humanity; in its outreach, between the wealthy and the destitute; and in its activities, between culture and commerce. This is a community that has fostered great social ideas like Amnesty International and famous international initiatives like the Academy of St Martin in the Fields. We are proud of our long history of beauty in our sanctuary and classical music, truth in our congregational life and work for justice and inclusion, and goodness in our walk with the homeless and the stranger. We're glad you are here, and we hope you soon share the warm spirit of this vibrant community.

Revd Dr Sam Wells
Vicar

Important Dates

c 334	After he shares his cloak with a beggar and Jesus appears to him in a dream, Roman soldier Martin is baptised in the Christian faith.
1222	First recorded reference to 'the Church and burial-place of St Martin' in London.
1542	London parish of St Martin's established and a new church built c 1544.
1726	James Gibbs' new St Martin-in-the-Fields completed at a cost of £36,000.
1914	Dick Sheppard is appointed Vicar of St Martin's and declares it the 'church of the ever-open door'.
1924	First radio broadcast of a church service takes place at St Martin's in January; later that year the *Christmas Appeal* is broadcast for the first time.
1948	Founding of the Social Care Unit.
1949	Free lunchtime concerts begin.
1958	The Academy of St Martin in the Fields founded by John Churchill, Master of Music at the church, and Neville Marriner.
1964	First service for the Chinese community held in the Dick Sheppard Chapel.
1984	Bishop Ho Ming Wah Chinese Community Centre opens at St Martin's.
2005–2008	£36m renewal project undertaken; the new East Window marks the final installation.

Who was St Martin?

Martin was born *c* 316 in Pannonia, today part of Hungary, and at 15 was enlisted into the Roman army. Posted to Amiens, in France, the young soldier rode through the city gate one bitter winter's night and came across an almost naked beggar. Martin dismounted his horse, cut his cloak in two with his sword and offered half to the beggar. That night, Christ, taking the form of the beggar, appeared to Martin in a dream and thanked him.

Shortly after, Martin was baptised and left the army; it was not permissible for a Christian to be a soldier because of the conflict between the military oath and the Church's teachings about peace.

While living as a recluse on an island near Ligugé, he founded a monastery – the first in France – to which he welcomed the sick and those excluded from society. It was here that it is thought Martin performed his first miracle.

The people of Tours were impressed by this holy man with healing powers, and when their bishop died they tricked Martin into visiting their town. Somewhat reluctantly he became their bishop, but continued his frugal lifestyle by living in caves outside the city.

Martin died on 8 November 397. Through his teachings many people came to Christ, and Martin became the first person to be made a saint who had not died a martyr. St Martin's Day is celebrated on 11 November, the day of his burial in the Cemetery of the Poor in Tours.

Patron saint of pacifists and soldiers

Although St Martin's patronage is linked to several fields, including beggars, tailors and innkeepers, he is also the patron saint of pacifists and the armed forces. His act of 'sharing the cloak' underpins the calling of St Martin-in-the-Fields to care for the poor and excluded, and to meet Christ in strangers by discovering the 'shared cloak' through its commercial activities.

Left: James Butler's statue of St Martin depicting the sharing of his cloak with the beggar.

The Early Churches

Excavations have revealed this site as sacred in Roman times, but the first recorded reference to 'the Church and burial-place of St Martin' comes in 1222. That 13th-century church was known as St Martin-nigh-the-Cross – a reference to a wooden cross in the village of Charing. It is likely to have been a small chapel, possibly used by pilgrims on their way to Westminster Abbey and by the monks working in the nearby convent (covent) garden. Over the next 300 years it acquired a steeple, tiled paving and three small chapels.

Above: 5th-century Roman sarcophagus unearthed during restoration work.

In the 16th century, Henry VIII – alarmed by coffins containing plague victims processing past his palace at Whitehall on their way to St Margaret's Westminster – decided the burials should take place at St Martin's, so made St Martin's a civil parish separate from St Margaret's.

The new parish, decreed in 1542, was mainly open fields, its southern boundary incorporating what is now Buckingham Palace. Around 1544 the old church was replaced with a new building. Its size – just 25 feet wide and 45 feet long – suggests its congregation was small. However by the 17th century the number of parishioners had increased considerably. As non-attendance at church was a punishable offence, the congregation continued growing and so the building was enlarged several times.

By 1660 the church was in a decayed state. With no funds for a new one, urgent repairs were carried out, including to the tower. In 1672 Christopher Wren, whose children were all baptised here, added a cupola. However, a survey in 1710 revealed that the walls were unable to support the roof. It was decided that the church – by now extended to 62 feet by 84 feet and with a 90-foot steeple with six bells – must be rebuilt. The last service was held on 11 June 1721.

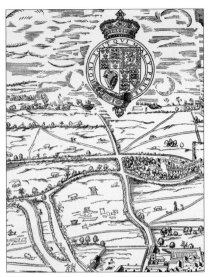

Above: St Martin-in-the-Fields c 1560. The Agas Map shows the original 13th-century Charing Cross with a tiny St Martin's nearby to the north-east.

An Eighteenth-Century Glory

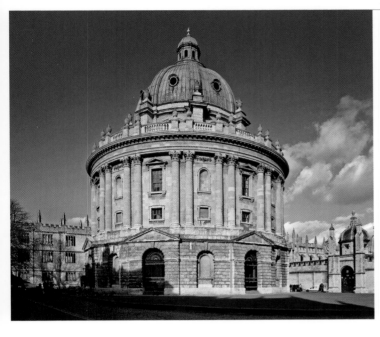

Left: The Radcliffe Camera, designed by James Gibbs for Oxford University and built 1737–49. It now houses part of the Bodleian Library.

Right: 18th-century print by Thomas Malton, showing the North face of St Martin-in-the-Fields.

NORTH FRONT OF S. MARTINS CHURCH

By the 18th century, St Martin's Lane – once a country path linking St Martin's to St Giles' (another church 'in the fields') – had become a fashionable, paved thoroughfare, home to a number of London's elite.

A new church at St Martin's was commissioned at the behest of George I, with James Gibbs appointed as architect and a budget of £22,000. The project was completed in 1726 at a cost eventually totalling £36,000.

The appearance of St Martin-in-the-Fields is so familiar that one can miss how dramatic its architectural statement was at the time. Gibbs' original suggestion was for a round, domed church entered through a portico, a shape that would have been in his mind considering he was about to submit plans for the new Radcliffe Camera in Oxford. The eventual smaller, rectangular design, with its 192-foot high steeple and classical temple front, fuses Baroque and Palladian styles. Upon its completion the building drew a mixed reception, although the new church became very fashionable and George I himself was appointed churchwarden.

Gibbs' blueprint

Gibbs' body of work had a profound effect. With few trained architects in the colonies in the 18th century, his major written work, *A Book of Architecture* (1728), became the most widely used pattern book for religious buildings in the English-speaking world. These include churches in such diverse places as Kolkata and Nova Scotia, but most particularly in the US where the closest replica to St Martin-in-the-Fields is St Paul's Chapel in downtown Manhattan.

Dick Sheppard

St Martin's is known as the 'church of the ever-open door', thanks to Canon H.R.L. (Dick) Sheppard, Vicar of St Martin's 1914–26.

Sheppard had long had a heart for those less fortunate than himself. When he was first ordained he worked in Bethnal Green, then one of London's most deprived areas.

It took much soul-searching for Dick to accept the position of Vicar at St Martin's. However, having spent a night in the parish talking to homeless people, he was persuaded that 'no square mile could provide a more thrilling or adventurous pitch.'

Right: Portrait of Dick Sheppard by Gerald Kelly, RA.

Before taking up his new post, in the early days of the First World War, Dick served as an army chaplain in the trenches. He was only there for a few weeks but the experience was transformative. In *H.R.L. Sheppard: Life and Letters*, his biographer R. Ellis Roberts tells of a vision Dick had while in Flanders:

> I stood on the west steps and saw what this church would be to the life of the people. They passed me, into its warm inside, hundreds and hundreds of all sorts of people, going up to the temple of their Lord, with all their difficulties, trials and sorrows. I saw it full of people, dropping in at all hours of the day and night. It was never dark, it was lighted all night and all day, and often tired bits of humanity swept in. And I said to them as they passed, 'Where are you going?' And they said only one thing, 'This is our home … This is St Martin's.'

With the war still raging in France, nearby Charing Cross station was the point of arrival and departure for many soldiers. On his return, Dick ensured that St Martin's and its crypt remained open around the clock: a refuge for those seeking shelter and food day or night. The doors have remained open ever since.

Above left: First World War soldiers pray in St Martin's before leaving for the trenches from Charing Cross.

Above right: The Dick Sheppard Chapel; a tapestry by Gerhard Richter hangs above the altar.

The Dick Sheppard Chapel

There is a chapel in the crypt named after the man who, like St Martin before him, had a Christian calling to help others. The Dick Sheppard Chapel is a quiet place in a busy city where visitors are welcome to reflect and pray.

Helping Homeless People

Above: Actress and broadcaster Felicity Finch, who plays Ruth Archer, supports the annual Christmas Appeal.

Above: Stephen was able to secure a home of his own, with support from the Vicar's Relief Fund.

Dick Sheppard's 'ever-open door' principle during the First World War set the pattern for St Martin's continuing care for the poor and vulnerable.

In the 1920s and 30s, unemployed ex-servicemen came with their families to receive meal tickets, hostel vouchers, food and clothing, or to sleep in the crypt. In 1948 the Welfare State was established. This was a partnership between government, churches and voluntary organisations. St Martin's recruited two full-time welfare workers and opened a Social Care Unit, which was soon helping thousands of people each year.

In 1973 St Martin's converted the former school into a day centre for young people and, during the 1980s, three existing organisations combined to form the London Connection, helping those aged 16–25.

In 2003 the Social Care Unit and London Connection merged to form The Connection at St Martin-in-the-Fields. With facilities close by, The Connection helps homeless people by providing specialist services – including a day and night centre, outreach for rough sleepers, skills training and career advice – to over 200 people in central London every day. In a friendly, welcoming environment, individuals are helped to address the issues that caused their homelessness and to gain the skills and confidence needed to make lasting changes in their lives.

One of the ways in which the work of Dick Sheppard continues is the ministry of the Sunday International Group. Started in 2013, it provides pastoral care and support for homeless people and asylum seekers who continue to find St Martin's a place of sanctuary every day of the year.

Above: Each May, since 1991, The Connection at St Martin's has organised a pilgrimage. Every year up to 100 walkers – including parishioners, homeless people and supporters – walk the 74-mile London-to-Canterbury pilgrimage in memory of Dick Sheppard, who is buried at Canterbury Cathedral, and raise funds for The Connection at St Martin's.

Broadcasting

Above: A broadcast from St Martin's, 1944.

It was John (later Lord) Reith of the BBC who first asked Dick Sheppard to broadcast a monthly service on the wireless, to make a connection between broadcasting and Christianity; the inaugural service was held at 6.15pm on 6 January 1924. It divided opinion around the world: there was a fan letter from a ship in the Suez Canal, while one priest was concerned that it might be heard by a man in a public house with his hat on. However, feedback was generally positive, and in 1927 the *Radio Times* publicised the services as bringing 'hope and comfort to many thousands of people who may never have seen the lofty spire of the famous London church.'

This broadcasting remains an important element in the life of St Martin's today, with regular broadcasts of BBC Radio 4's *Sunday Worship*, *Daily Service* and other special events. From the Second World War, when secret radios were used to listen to services from behind enemy lines, to modern-day broadcasts using the latest technology and reaching all corners of the globe, St Martin's continues to play an integral part in the work of the worldwide church.

Christmas Appeal

With his broadcasts reaching a wide audience, in 1924 Dick Sheppard founded the Christmas Fund to raise money for disadvantaged people. This fundraising activity grew under his successor – Pat McCormick, Vicar of St Martin's 1927–40 – who became the first clergyman to be televised, during a five-minute slot after the King's Speech on Christmas Day 1937. The Appeal (now the *BBC Radio 4 Christmas Appeal with St Martin-in-the-Fields*) is still broadcast annually, raising over £2m a year and benefitting homeless and vulnerable people all over the country.

Above: Hugh Dennis, a supporter of the BBC Radio 4 Christmas Appeal with St Martin-in-the-Fields, *during a recording for broadcast.*

Facing New Challenges

In 1987 the church faced a crisis. For too long it had relied on legacy income and the benefaction of wealthy associates. Its fabric was weakening and its revenue stream was fragile. It faced bankruptcy. Revd Geoffrey Brown convened a group of people and they devised the Enterprise – setting up a café and shop below ground as well as expanding the church's commercial concert programme. Initially it proved hard to reconcile the congregation's aspirations with the realities of profit-making in an unyielding business environment. Gradually understanding grew and St Martin's added commercial expertise to its existing reputation in congregational life, broadcasting, social care, campaigning and music.

The community began to reflect on issues such as good employment practice, cherishing a staff team, meeting customer needs and working as one organisation. These issues currently also include questions of environmental sustainability, fair trade and the living wage.

Today there is an enlarged Café in the Crypt, an outdoor seasonal Café in the Courtyard, a thriving gift shop, a brass-rubbing centre, an extensive events programme and one of the busiest concert lists in the country. From having been an organisation that protested against what was wrong in society and upheld the disadvantaged, St Martin's has become also a community that seeks to practise good and healthy ways to create wealth and to do business.

Above: The Crypt now hosts a thriving café that is open every day except Christmas Day and Boxing Day. All proceeds support the work of St Martin's.

Into the Twenty-first Century

Following in his entrepreneurial predecessor's wake, Nicholas Holtam (Vicar 1995–2011) progressed what Canon Brown had started and in 2005 began one of the most notable achievements in St Martin's history: a £36m renewal project 'for the common good in service of humanity to the greater glory of God'. Completed in 2008, supported by its patron HRH The Prince of Wales and thousands of people giving prayerful and financial support, the project resulted in many advances at the church, and won several awards in the areas of architecture, regeneration and heritage.

It saw James Gibbs' 18th-century masterpiece completely restored for the first time: this included removing floors installed by the Victorians in order to reinstate the original height of the interior and allow natural light to flood in, and reordering the sanctuary to give greater flexibility for worship and concerts.

Perhaps the most inspired dimension of this major renovation saw the precincts of St Martin's ingeniously extended by Eric Parry Architects, with many of the changes taking place underground. The circular glass pavilion alongside the church descends to a foyer leading to the box office, gift shop, brass-rubbing centre, meeting rooms, offices, music rehearsal rooms, the Bishop Ho Ming Wah Chinese Community Centre, the Dick Sheppard Chapel and the immensely popular Café in the Crypt. The renewal also provided purpose-built facilities for The Connection at St Martin's for its work with homeless and vulnerable people.

The creation of these spaces will serve the church and the community for generations to come.

Far left: St Martin's 192-foot spire, clad in scaffolding during the restoration project.

Left: HRH Prince Charles at the topping-out ceremony marking the completion of the project.

Treasures of St Martin's

St Martin-in-the-Fields is a Grade I listed building. Not only is its exterior an imposing part of the landscape of Trafalgar Square, but the interior of the church also contains many treasures, both historic and modern.

Bells

By the early 16th century the church had three bells, plus a Sanctus bell. A new set of bells was hung in 1539, and in 1583 eight new bells were cast. When Gibbs' new church was built these were recast and another four added; re-hung in 1912, they were set too high and difficult to ring. In 1984 it was decided to replace them and the new bells of St Martin's, cast by Whitechapel Bell Foundry, were installed in 1988, hung a stage lower than their predecessors to make ringing easier.

Oranges and Lemons

Many people know the nursery rhyme *Oranges and Lemons* and the line: '"I owe you five farthings," say the bells of St Martin's.' At one time there were five churches dedicated to St Martin within the square mile of the City of London and it is debatable to which one the rhyme refers – but as it was written in the mid-18th century and St Martin-in-the-Fields has been standing much longer, it is not unreasonable for this St Martin's to stake its claim.

Chinese letters in the sanctuary

Benches in the sanctuary are decorated with four pairs of carved letters: Chinese characters representing Faith (shown right), Hope, Love and Wisdom. Wisdom is held in high esteem in Chinese culture. It is also one of the feminine characteristics of God described in the Old Testament.

Font

The font where so many have begun their Christian journey dates from 1689 and came from the earlier church. It was donated by William Bridgeman – a parishioner and Joint Secretary of the Admiralty in Whitehall – as a thank-offering for his son, born after 20 years of marriage. The decorative white marble pedestal supports an oval basin in coloured marble. Its carved oak cover (not on display) was sold in 1845 by a churchwarden who considered it to be of little value; fortunately it was later recovered from an antique dealer.

Pulpit

Today's preachers still reach the platform of the oak pulpit via a carved staircase to stand 6 feet above the congregation. Probably designed by James Gibbs and made locally by one of the furniture makers in St Martin's Lane, the pulpit was then a 'triple decker' and situated in the north aisle. Renovations by William Gilson Humphry (Vicar 1855–86) saw the pulpit repositioned and its elaborate sounding board, reading desk and clerk's pew removed. The 2008 renewal project relocated the pulpit once more, improving sight lines for all audiences and moving it closer to where it is thought to have been originally located.

Gallery boxes

Behind one of the windows at gallery level is the Royal Box, with a fireplace and comfortable chairs. The last person to use it regularly was Queen Mary (1867–1953); not amused when the vicar suggested the stairs to the Royal Box were rather steep and that Her Majesty might prefer to sit in a chair in front of the pews, she responded, 'I come to worship the Almighty, not to be stared at.'

Nave ceiling

Visitors standing in the nave of St Martin's only need to glance up to revel in one of its enduring glories: the Baroque ceiling. It is divided into panels decorated with cherubim, clouds, shells and scrolls; the work of Italian artists Signori Artari and Bagutti who created a 'thin place' where we catch a glimpse of heaven.

Royal coat of arms

St Martin-in-the-Fields has long had links with the Royal Family, being the parish church of both Buckingham Palace and St James's Palace. Not only did George I serve as churchwarden, but the Queen Mother was the first patron of the Friends of St Martin-in-the-Fields, formed in the 1950s, and visited the church often.

It is no surprise that the link to the monarchy is reflected in the particularly fine Royal coat of arms in the nave. Beneath the crest, supported by a unicorn and a lion, is the motto of the British sovereign: DIEU ET MON DROIT, which translates as 'God and my right'.

East Window

The renowned East Window, the final installation of the 2008 renewal project, is one of the most significant pieces of religious art commissioned in modern times. The abstract cross, lit to form a focal point visible both internally and externally, is by Shirazeh Houshiary and her architect husband, Pip Horne. The design emphasises James Gibbs' original intention for St Martin's to be filled with light – a key theme throughout the renewal programme.

The brief for the window suggested Jacob's ladder as a starting point, a narrative that has a theme of uniting both heaven and earth. On 20 October 1726 at the consecration of the new church, Vicar Dr Zechariah Pearce preached from Genesis 28 – the story of Jacob's ladder – including verse 17, which concludes: 'This is none other than the house of God, and this is the gate of heaven.'

Above: The new altar, designed by Shirazeh Houshiary and Pip Horne.

Altar

In 2008 Shirazeh Houshiary and Pip Horne were also responsible for creating the new altar, the focus of the nave. Created from a single hollowed-out travertine block set on a dark oak base, its simplicity complements the intricate design of the East Window and beautifully captures the sense of living stone the artists were striving for: monumental yet fragile.

Shekinah

Above the altar in the place of glory lies the Shekinah, the Hebrew word for the presence of God. In the Old Testament, this is the mystery of God that appeared, for example, to Moses in the burning bush. In the New Testament, the notion, associated with a cloud, reappears – for example at the Transfiguration, when the Father's voice announces, 'This is my beloved Son: listen to him.' The four Hebrew letters spell out the name of God, which is so holy that Jews don't utter it. In English it is usually spelt Yahweh.

Processional cross

A new processional cross was dedicated in 2013. It is the work of sculptor Brian Catling and is formed from just two pieces of wood joined with string. The contorted shape of the piece expresses the poverty and agony of the cross, whilst its casting in aluminium and gilding of white gold is a reminder that our suffering and failures will be redeemed. A strip of cloth attached to the cross incorporates the story of St Martin coming to Christ after sharing his cloak with a beggar.

Sanctuary mosaics

Creating an additional focus on either side of the sanctuary are two Victorian mosaics. They depict the annunciation – the moment the angel announced to Mary that she had been chosen to bear the Son of God.

Right: Bronze sculpture commemorating Hector Pieterson, by Chaim Stephenson.

Victims of Injustice and Violence

This bronze sculpture, a memorial to the anti-apartheid movement, depicts a young man carrying a dead child. It is by Chaim Stephenson, inspired by a photograph taken after the shooting of 13-year-old Hector Pieterson in Soweto in 1976. The artwork was dedicated at St Martin's in 1994 by Archbishop Desmond Tutu, who described the pain and struggle of his people to sustain their faith in a brighter future during 46 years of apartheid. The current Vicar, Revd Dr Sam Wells, preached at the dedication of the replica of this statue at St Mary's Cathedral in Johannesburg in 2015.

Revd Dr Sam Wells presents Revd Richard Carter to HM the Queen following a service of remembrance at St Martin-in-the-Fields marking the 70th Anniversary of VJ Day.

FEPOW memorial

In the north-west corner of the church there is a memorial for those who died as prisoners of war or as civilian internees while in Japanese hands between 1941 and 1945, and for those who died subsequently as a result of their sufferings during captivity.

In the Beginning

At the entrance to St Martin's is a striking sculpture, *In the Beginning*, commissioned to be in place of the traditional Christmas crib to mark the new millennium and modelled on a member of the congregation. It was carved from a 4.5-tonne block of Portland stone by artist Mike Chapman, who said of the piece: 'It seemed to me that a tiny life-size baby carved from stone in such an enormous environment would be the best way to remind us all of just whose birthday we are celebrating.'

Saint John's Bible

Started in 1998, it took eleven years for the only Bible to be handwritten since the advent of the printing press to be completed. Commissioned by Benedictine monks in Minnesota, where the original is kept, the Saint John's Bible was created by a team of artists in Monmouthshire, directed by Donald Jackson, calligrapher to HM the Queen.

Nativity

Since 2006 St Martin-in-the-Fields' nativity scene has been installed in Trafalgar Square each December. This is the work of Tomoaki Suzuki who carved the 40 percent life-size grouping from limewood, his inspiration taken from St Martin's multicultural community, and the figures clothed by fashion designer Jessica Ogden.

St Martin's holds one of only 299 facsimile copies of this seven-volume work of art and theology, which is used weekly in Sunday morning worship. The first copy was presented to the Pope and the second to St Martin's.

Paintings

Four paintings of particular significance in the church are:
✦ *King George I* by the Studio of Kneller, *c* 1716. This was probably obtained in recognition of the monarch's generosity towards his parish church.
✦ *St Martin and the Beggar* by Francesco Solimena. Thought to be 18th century, this is a version of a wall painting in the monastery of St Martin, near Naples. The beggar is depicted as the perfect human being, Jesus Christ.
✦ *James Gibbs* by Andrea Soldi, given to St Martin's in 1800. The architect is shown with his *Book of Architecture*; in the background are plans for a circular building – probably the Radcliffe Camera in Oxford, rather than his original plan for St Martin's.
✦ *Dick Sheppard* by Gerald Kelly (see page 6). Kelly was one of the finest portrait artists of his day.

Working in Partnership

St Martin's desire to help people from all walks of life is reflected in its commitment to assisting those less fortunate in London and all corners of the world.

The Least, the Last and the Lost

While St Martin's is famous for its work with homeless people, it has several other associations with issues of justice and disadvantage. It was here in 1960 that the idea was born for Amnesty International, the global movement of solidarity with prisoners of conscience. A young lawyer, Peter Benenson, had been angered after learning about two Portuguese students imprisoned for drinking a toast to liberty in a Lisbon café. He later said: 'That so enraged me that I walked up the steps of St Martin-in-the-Fields, out of the Underground, and went in to see what could really be done effectively to mobilise world opinion'. In May 1961 he wrote in *The Observer* about the plight of 'forgotten prisoners', appealing to individuals to take action. Lighting a candle in St Martin-in-the-Fields to mark the 20th anniversary of Amnesty, Benenson said: 'I have lit this candle, in the words of Shakespeare, "against oblivion" – so that the forgotten prisoners should always be remembered. We work in Amnesty against oblivion.'

Above: Peter Benenson lighting a candle outside St Martin's to celebrate Amnesty's 20th anniversary

Other imaginative and courageous social ideas have been incubated at St Martin's. It was in what is today the study of Revd Dr Sam Wells (who became the vicar here in 2012) that the National Council for Civil Liberties – today known as Liberty – first met. Shelter, which helps those struggling with bad housing or homelessness, was launched here, as was *The Big Issue* – the magazine written, published and sold by homeless and long-term unemployed people.

The church has a close connection with Christian Aid, founded as Christian Reconstruction in Europe in the aftermath of the Second World War, its purpose to alleviate the suffering of ordinary people, no matter what their faith. During the first Christian Aid Week in 1957 a replica refugee camp was erected at St Martin's, vividly depicting the plight of refugees.

London's 'Pearlies'

The church has enjoyed a long association with London's other 'royal family': the Pearly kings and queens. Founded by Henry Croft in 1875, they are renowned for their fundraising for the vulnerable. The Original Pearly Kings and Queens Association has been associated with St Martin's since 1956. Their celebration of Harvest Festival in October is always a glittering occasion.

The world's parish church

In the 18th century St Martin-in-the-Fields was one of the churches involved in founding the Church of England's many overseas mission societies. A freed slave – whose autobiography, *The Interesting Narrative of the Life of Olaudah Equiano* (1789), depicted the horrors of slavery and was influential in the passing of the Slave Trade Act 1807 – lived in London and worshipped here. In the same tradition, sanctuary was provided in the 20th century to Jewish refugees.

The regular acts of worship broadcast on the BBC World Service made St Martin's world-famous. There is a legend of Revd Austen Williams entering a West African home in the 1950s and the host saying, 'Look, it's the vicar!' Such fame has made St Martin's a place of pilgrimage for Christians from around the globe, a tradition that continues to this day.

St Martin's association with South Africa arose because the South African High Commission is its next-door neighbour. During the apartheid era, there were frequent demonstrations outside South Africa House. Members of St Martin's actively participated and supported the movement. In 2013 the church was proud to host services of thanksgiving for the life of former South African president Nelson Mandela.

Above and left: St Martin's hosted a thanksgiving service for Nelson Mandela in partnership with the South African High Commission.

In a Radio 4 broadcast from St Martin's, the Archbishop of Canterbury said, 'Mandela had the capacity not only to have a vision for reconciliation, to combine courage and forgiveness in the most extraordinary alchemy of humanity but he also had a remarkable gift for turning that into practice.'

St Martin's links across the world remain important today. Relations with such places as Malawi and Solomon Islands are strong. Many visitors come from the United States: the Bishop of New York led the groundbreaking ceremony in February 2006 marking the start of building for the renewal project.

Hong Kong and China

One of St Martin's most important roles in recent times has been to provide social care and a meeting place for members of London's Chinese community. For over 50 years the church has been home to an active Cantonese-speaking congregation, which today has its own Church Council and associate vicar. In more recent times, this has extended to include a Mandarin-speaking congregation, and every Sunday there are services in both Cantonese and Mandarin.

St Martin-in-the-Fields also houses the Bishop Ho Ming Wah Association and Community Centre. In 1964 Ronald Owen Hall (Ho Ming Wah in Chinese), Bishop of Hong Kong and Macau 1932–66, asked social worker and priest Revd Shui Ying Lee to work with Chinese restaurant workers living in Soho. As well as holding a service in Cantonese, 'SY' counselled those struggling with life in a strange land while they worked hard to send money to their families in Hong Kong. With a growing Chinese population, the Ho Ming Wah opened in 1987 and today welcomes 150 people each week. Supporters in Hong Kong helped financially when the Association was first founded and were generous in their contributions when the Centre was relocated during the renewal project.

Commonwealth Day Observance
In 1966 St Martin's hosted the first Commonwealth Day Observance, bringing together people of different faiths and nationalities for the first Affirmation of Faith service, attended by HM Queen Elizabeth II and HRH Prince Philip. Despite a storm of protest and debate, and thanks to intervention by the Queen and the Dean of Westminster, it has continued ever since.

Above: Members of the Chinese congregation celebrate its Golden Jubilee in 2014.

Music at St Martin's

For many people the heart of St Martin-in-the-Fields is its prestigious musical heritage. It is believed that there was an organ at the church before 1500; its replacement – the Schreider organ of 1727 – was funded by George I and is thought to have been played by Handel.

Free lunchtime concerts, given by young and upcoming musicians three times a week, have been enriching the London musical community since 1949. In 1958 the now internationally famous orchestra – the Academy of St Martin in the Fields – was founded at the church. Directed by Sir Neville Marriner until 2011 and specialising in performances of Baroque repertoire, the Academy still enjoys a close relationship with St Martin's.

St Martin's is one of the country's busiest concert venues: there are over 350 concerts here every year performed by both external performers (including the popular Jazz Nights in the Café in the Crypt) and internal musical groups (the flourishing Sound of St Martin's concert series).

Thanks to the church's long-established broadcasting tradition, its music has a worldwide reach: St Martin-in-the-Fields is a must-visit concert venue for classical music fans visiting London, and Trafalgar Square passers-by stop to marvel at the church they have heard mentioned in concert broadcasts on the radio.

Above and right: The organ at St Martin-in-the-Fields built by J.W. Walker & Sons in 1990. It is considered to be one of the finest in London and received the Carpenters' Award for the quality of its casework.

St Martin-in-the-Fields is justly proud of its reputation for nurturing the development of young musical talent and for supporting musicians at the start of their careers. The lunchtime concerts are a covetable opportunity for young performers (often from the London conservatoires). The Chamber Music Competition, founded in 2010, has quickly become a fixture in the St Martin's calendar, and offers practical support to its prize-winners through a series of professional engagements.

The musical activity at St Martin's is very wide and varied. Audiences around the world associate the name St Martin-in-the-Fields with high-quality music-making. As plans develop for further work with young musicians, the rich musical tradition continues to expand.

Choirs at St Martin's

St Martin's is well-known for its vocal ensembles and its work with young singers. It supports a number of high-quality voluntary choirs: the Choir of St Martin-in-the-Fields, which sings at Sunday services and at high-profile events, broadcasts and concerts; the Occasional Singers, who perform at St Martin's about once a month; the Children's Voices of St Martin's, which was founded in 2014 for 7–13 year olds and continues to grow from strength to strength; and St Martin's Chorus, which was founded in 2015 as a project-based choir for voluntary singers. There is also an in-demand Choral Scholarship scheme – open, unlike many similar programmes, to both men and women – that supports the development of aspiring singers at Wednesday services and beyond. Additionally, a young professional choir, St Martin's Voices, has developed rapidly in recent years: the group performs ambitious repertoire in concert, has made numerous recordings and podcasts, and has featured on *Choral Evensong* on BBC Radio 3. Every Thursday St Martin's Voices and Revd Dr Sam Wells present an exploration of the music of our religious heritage in the immensely popular lunchtime series *Great Sacred Music*.

The Crypt

By 1853, no further interments were allowed in the crypt at St Martin's. The vaults were cleared and many of the coffins removed, although some remained until 1938 when these too were re-interred. During the Second World War the crypt became an air-raid shelter.

Above: Dedicated to Elizabeth Macdowall, who died in 1670 aged 30, the memorial 'recommends this marble to her memory and her example to all worthy weomen' (sic).

On the walls and pillars in the crypt are a number of coats of arms and memorial plaques. Many are from the previous church; the oldest, inscribed to one Thomas Evans, goes back to Elizabethan times. The roughly carved whipping post (left) – dating from 1752 – was used outside in Trafalgar Square for a routine form of corporal punishment not revoked until 1837.

Nell Gwyn

Famous burials at St Martin's include that of Nell Gwyn, Charles II's mistress, who died in 1687 and left money to the church, including £100 for 'clothes for the winter and such other necessaries' for the poorest of the parishioners.

No Ordinary Parish

St Martin-in-the-Fields is a unique configuration of cultural, charitable and commercial initiatives rooted in the life of a vibrant Church of England congregation.

At the centre of its life is worship of the Trinity: Father, Son and Holy Spirit. There are grand choral services, notably the Parish Eucharist on Sunday mornings; there are quieter, more intimate gatherings, often in the Dick Sheppard Chapel; and there is an array of special services. These occasions include civic ceremonies such as the Victoria Cross and George Cross service, honouring courageous and selfless duty; annual gatherings like the Coutts service and the Farmers Club Harvest Festival; and personal moments such as memorial services and weddings.

Among these, perhaps the most poignant are a pattern of acute pastoral services: for those who have died homeless, for missing people, for victims of homicide, and for those affected by suicide. It is central to St Martin's vocation to stand alongside people as they discover words to say, and begin to perceive beauty and meaning even in the face of horror and tragedy.

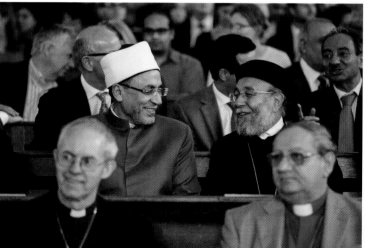

Above: Service commemorating the homeless; memorial doves are placed on the flag to signify those lost.

Left: The Archbishop of Canterbury and the Bishop of Egypt at the launch of 'The Bridge', an interfaith art exhibition at St Martin's.

In similar ways, the congregation is consistently renewed by deeper encounters with the suffering of disability and conditions such as mental illness and dementia. It has a special heart for those who have known exclusion on the grounds of sexual orientation or rejection on account of their migrant status. Its education programmes draw wide and diverse audiences and consider the interface of faith with violence, story, ecology, exclusion and community. There are more devotional programmes during Advent and Lent, and a lively pattern of study groups, retreats, away days and parish weekends. Healing, pastoral care and fellowship are central to the congregation's sense of mutual well-being. Concern for human dignity, fair trade and environmental sustainability are constant causes for reflection and engagement.

Within the geographical parish of St Martin-in-the-Fields lie both Buckingham Palace and 10 Downing Street. Thus, members of the congregation are always aware of a vocation well beyond their own lives. The regular broadcasts and the myriad of people who see St Martin's as their place of identification and belonging when in London makes this no ordinary parish: never less than a parish church, but often much more.

Left: Brothers from the Melanesian Mission dance before the altar; St Martin's has strong links with Solomon Islands.

Below: St Martin's Nativity play performed by the congregation.

We hope you've enjoyed your visit to St Martin's.
If you want to help secure our future, please
support Building Futures, our £4.5m campaign
to preserve the historic buildings and all that
is achieved here. Please donate at:
www.smitf.org/support-us. Thank you.

For details of services, concerts and other activities at
St Martin-in-the-Fields, please visit the website
www.stmartin-in-the-fields.org
or telephone 020 7766 1100.

St Martin-in-the-Fields, Trafalgar Square, London WC2N 4JJ

Acknowledgements

Text by Gill Knappett, with contributions from Revd Dr Sam Wells
and Alice Usher.
Edited by Claire Handy.
Designed by Jemma Cox.

All images © St Martin-in-the-Fields, except for: © Marc Gascoigne:
pp.1, 8, 13, 16, 23, 24, 25, 28, 30, 31 & 52; Pitkin Publishing: p.5; ©
Chetan Pawan: p.8; © David Lindsay: pp.8 & 14; reproduced by kind
permission of Hugh Dennis and © Marc Gascoigne: p.9; © Phil Ashley:
pp.10 & 29; © Mike Doherty: p.11; LA(Phot) Iggy Roberts/Crown
Copyright: p.20; © Raould Shade: p.22; © Liam Bailey: pp.26 & 27.

Photography by Heather Hook © St Martin-in-the-Fields: pp.2, 3, 6, 7,
12, 13, 14, 15, 16, 17, 18–19, 20, 21 & 27.

The publisher wishes to thank the many people of St Martin-in-the-Fields
involved in the preparation of this guidebook.

Acknowledgement is particularly given to *St Martin-in-the-Fields* by
Malcolm Johnson (published by Phillimore/The History Press) and the
church website, which have been used for reference in the preparation of
this guidebook.

ISBN: 978-1-84165-622-9   1/15

£5.99

PITKIN

ISBN: 978-1-84165-622-9

9 781841 656229